Sprouted Soul

Whole-Souled Poems

~ by Doobie

Dedication

Gratefully dedicated to my dear wife Vicky, my inspiration and my true love.

And to everyone who has been on a quest,

For inner peace at times of grief,

For gratifying bliss and emerging belief,

For rising hopes when struggling to cope,

For soothing your soul during seasons of fall,

To enlighten mystical love, to awaken your call.

~Doobie

Contents

~ *Unmasked* ~

Soul to Soul, bare it all,

Evolve, do not hide, obey your call,

Oh, mighty divine do not let me fall.

Unmasked, our spirits unfold,

Soul to Soul embrace, behold.

~ *Fearless* ~

Set me free, oh, heavenly Soul,

Let me be, I may fall,

Broken winged, I stumble, I crawl,

Lightning fights dark shadows, bow wicked foe,

Fearless, no sorrows, I follow my call.

~ Sprouted ~

Her sprouted Soul eternally grows,

Her pathways manifest for them to follow,

Resiliently she struggles upstream as she flows,

Humbly she enlightens, inspires them all,

Oh, sacred spirit, guard her ways for she is

Our strength, our sole hope.

~ *Hero* ~

Dark sky, troubled heart trapped by clouds,

Sapphire waves, uncovered mind trapped in the sounds,

Oh, Holy man, enlighten me, guide me to my call,

Eyes shut, embrace my heart, light up my Soul,

Who is the hero who will not fall?

~ Sail ~

Lay down your hands, acceptance in still,

Embrace faith, blessed in peace,

No Soul is left alone, a new dawn is born,

Sail on the river of light, oh graceful one,

No more doubts, your devoted son.

~ *Divine* ~

Smooth as the tender tones of a flute,

As they pierce each cell, pave each route,

Peace is their only way,

Savor Divine love like a sweet fruit,

Bare, share, pray, and bloom.

~ *Forgive* ~

From all that was to be taken or given,

From all that was done with mistreat,

Nothing is left, nothing to be scripted,

Embrace on your Soul, and forgive,

For only Love will subsist, for only Love will defeat.

~ *Soul* ~

Falling leaves shelter my tears,

Heart numbed, love has gone,

Wandering clouds, outshine my fears,

Bare Soul has taken it all,

Oh, Great Spirit lead me to awakening dawn.

~ Child ~

Oh, noble one, I just want to be me,

Oh, Holy Spirit, I just want to be free,

Let it go, search no more,

Be grateful... just be,

Embrace your Soul, accept your destiny,

Live! You are a child of eternity.

~ *Change* ~

Deceitful sight, we are lost, out of place,

Soulful nature, enfolded with beauty and grace,

Eyes shut, breath deep... exhale,

Change has come, delightful embrace,

We are one, nature - Mother Earth.

~ Beloved ~

And now that we are one,

We left all that has gone,

Bonded Love embraces our Souls till the end time,

Oh, my angel, my beloved, lay your hand in mine,

Now that we are one, we sail to the never ebbing sun.

~ Careless ~

Her Soul softly rose upon enchanting sound,

Trailing her destiny, she glides through rivers of clouds,

It is written; it is destined, could it be undone?

Careless heart, she marches, abandoning all doubts,

Inner call, her only guidance,

Awakens Soul in the break of dawn.

~ *Angel* ~

Blow your wings over my shadow,

Touch my soul, bless me, I will follow,

Oh, angel of mercy, angel of despair,

Guide me out of the valley of sorrow,

Escort me to the land of tomorrow.

~ *Bless* ~

Soaring prayers pierced the misty dawn,

Soundless tears sheltered, a Soul is born,

Child caressed in awakening pale light,

Bless his path, relish his soul, oh, Mighty One,

Hands reached, angels smiled, Love has won.

~ *Fall* ~

When our Ego let us believe,

We know it all, nothing is left to achieve,

Our life seems in order, in false-centered selves.

Then, it is time to turn to our Soul,

Time to step forward, to say it all,

For it is this turning that determines,

Do we remain or fall.

~ *Bliss* ~

Humble, yet fearless, I walk alone,

Obey no master, I follow no Don,

Oh, heavenly ray guide me home!

Where blissful havens shield our Souls,

Where we are One, bounded by mystic veils.

~ *Humble* ~

Often she drifts confused, in painful disbelief,

"Why?" She asks, tormented in grief,

Would she ever know?

Would she ever comprehend?

Humble, eyes closed, she prays and reaches out her hands.

~ *Bow* ~

She fights evil darkness, triumphs over wicked Souls,

She defeats dragons, pierces the wings of mighty foes,

Divine spirits shelter her as she flows upon heavenly storms,

Her heart nests amid mercy, hopes in her bare sword,

Humble, I bow, I follow and obey her call.

~ *Exhale* ~

Lost Soul journeys, mysteries unfold,

Frozen winding roads, fated stories to be told,

Breathe, mystical light awakening the inner call,

Exhale, heaven is her comfort and relief,

Milky Way illuminates her footsteps... she leaves.

~ *Prayers* ~

Silence, sorrow has landed, weep holy ground,

Hurtful breeze had blown, memories had shaded and gone,

Soul searches mate, none found,

Oh, heavenly spirit, do not let hopes be downed,

Carry my prayers, for my beloved and I unbound.

~ Peace ~

And the crowd roars, worshiping the hero,

Above she stands erect, her gaze piercing lost souls,

And the crowd bows, obeys the idol,

Behold, she rises, her voice thunderously falls,

And the crowd howls, swords and arrows,

"Peace!" Her bleeding heart sheds hidden sorrow.

~ *Journey* ~

A lonesome Soul, searches for her call,

Light sparkles over her life's journey on the rise,

Deceitful "helpers," oh yes, they know it all,

Never will she please them, nor fulfill chatted yearnings,

For it is her life's journey, only she bears the toll.

~ Destined ~

Carry me to my divine goal,

Guide me to a sheltered shore,

Bless my pathway amid petal of rose,

Unleash my mind, unseal the door,

For I am a drifting Soul, destined to where the wind blows.

~ *Ocean* ~

Scars deeply rooted, flesh and bones were bared,

Wounded heart, sorrow and despair,

Delightful times of gladness and bliss, she shared,

Glorious moments of joy, she was blessed.

She sails on an ocean of love, cherish, and care.

~ Namaste ~

Bliss in her veins eternity flows,

Dare she share it with lovers and foes,

Human's heart is a mystery unsolved,

Nature's art is her inner world,

Gentle Soul, her fragile wings blow,

"Namaste," she whispers as her faithful heart glows.

~ *Pretense* ~

Agonizing lessons yet to be learned,

Bewildered, she wonders, will it ever end?

Fragile soul, captivated in a world of pretense,

Ample solitude bounded, she reaches bare hand,

As she surrendered her hopeful journey to the Promised Land.

~ *Boundless* ~

Harmony is my aspiration, serenity is my passion,

Heavenly nature's sounds, I surrender, astound,

Reveal my inner light, glow with glorious delight,

Boundless love in my heart, I submit to the unknown,

For I know my beloved, I am not alone.

~ *Passion* ~

Lonely she paces, unattended void she left behind,

Gracefully she struggles, lasting rules she redefines,

Graciously she races, inexorable desires unbind,

Cautiously she guards, encounters the unconfined,

Heroically she leads upon a path of passion,

Immensely in the stillness she unwinds.

~ *Hopes* ~

When nothing ever seems to be better,

When you are down and nights getting colder,

Cling to your dreams, transcending hearts and Souls,

Everlasting hopes flow where the wild river falls,

Eternal spring overshadows and embraces our whole.

~ *Rainbow* ~

Be at peace divine Soul,

Circled bright light, as the night falls,

Wordlessly she prayers, echoes in solitary halls,

Tides raise darkness, as the angel calls,

Distant rainbow awakens dreams and hopes.

~ *Whole* ~

Drowned in deep sadness, bathed in sea of despair,

Struggles to trust her faith, accepts her loss,

Fights to live her life, nurtures her hope,

Sacred spirit, take her hand, guide her to a safe shore,

For her Soul knows it all, her whole, her call.

~ *Dare* ~

When your pain is too hard to bear,

Broken heart, seems as if no one cares,

Precious moments embraced with prayers,

Hold on to the One, and share,

Sprouted smile strives to live, to dare.

~ *Canvas* ~

Her laughter slowly died, deep darkness covered the wall,

Wishes diminished, buried under ashes black as coal,

Mystical journey carries her toward her goal,

Nature guides her through the light into a whole,

Beloved soul-mate reveals the canvas of her soul.

~ *Grace* ~

Darkness - her Soul eclipses under dusky space,

Blazing sorrow spears her veins, leaves no trace,

Dawn breaks, first sunbeam tenderly glows upon her face,

Faithfully she prays, hopes drift over the holy place,

Lightness - her devotion shines through, inspired by celestial grace.

Connect with Doobie:

www.sproutedsoul.net

www.facebook.com/SproutedSoul

Twitter: @Doobie_Shemer

Kindle: www.amazon.com/dp/B00I5VUPTW